AF228549

MASERATI

A&D Xtreme
BOLD HI-LO NONFICTION
An imprint of Abdo Publishing
abdobooks.com

S.L. HAMILTON

TAKE IT TO THE XTREME!

GET READY FOR AN XTREME ADVENTURE!
THE PAGES OF THIS BOOK WILL TAKE YOU INTO
THE THRILLING WORLD OF MASERATI.
WHEN YOU HAVE FINISHED READING THIS BOOK, TAKE THE
XTREME CHALLENGE ON PAGE 45 ABOUT WHAT YOU'VE LEARNED!

ABDOBOOKS.COM

Published by Abdo Publishing, a division of ABDO, PO Box 398166, Minneapolis, Minnesota 55439. Copyright © 2023 by Abdo Consulting Group, Inc. International copyrights reserved in all countries. No part of this book may be reproduced in any form without written permission from the publisher. A&D Xtreme™ is a trademark and logo of Abdo Publishing.

052022
092022

THIS BOOK CONTAINS RECYCLED MATERIALS

Editor: John Hamilton

Copy Editor: Tamara L. Britton

Graphic Design: Sue Hamilton

Cover Design: Laura Graphenteen

Cover Photo: Shutterstock

Interior Photos & Illustrations: All photos Maserati S.p.A., except: Alamy-pgs 10-11 & 16-17; AP-pgs 14-15; iStock-pgs 22-23; Library of Congress-pgs 12 & 13; Shutterstock-pgs 4-5 & 9 (fountain); Wikimedia-pgs 6-7.

LIBRARY OF CONGRESS CONTROL NUMBER: 2021942762

PUBLISHER'S CATALOGING-IN-PUBLICATION DATA

Names: Hamilton, S.L., author.

Title: Maserati / by S.L. Hamilton

Description: Minneapolis, Minnesota : Abdo Publishing, 2023 | Series: Xtreme cars | Includes online resources and index.

Identifiers: ISBN 9781532196089 (lib. bdg.) | ISBN 9781098217013 (ebook)

Subjects: LCSH: Maserati automobiles--Juvenile literature. | Sports cars--Juvenile literature. | Cars (Automobiles)--Juvenile literature.

Classification: DDC 629.2221--dc23

TABLE OF
CONTENTS

ITALIAN LUXURY & POWER

Maserati has created world-renowned automobiles for more than 100 years. The Italian cars are known for their power and style, surrounding drivers and passengers in the ultimate combination of speed and **luxury**.

HISTORY OF MASERATI

The Maserati company was started in 1914 by Italian engineer and racer Alfieri Maserati, together with his brothers Ettore and Ernesto. Only months later, World War I began. The Maserati brothers joined the war effort, creating improved **spark plugs** for aircraft engines.

Alfieri Maserati

After the war, the Maserati brothers returned to their shop in Bologna, Italy. Their first car was the Maserati Tipo 26, a **Grand Prix** racing car built from 1926-1932.

A Maserati Tipo 26. *Tipo* is Italian for "type" or "model."

The Maserati logo
was placed in an
oval in 1951.

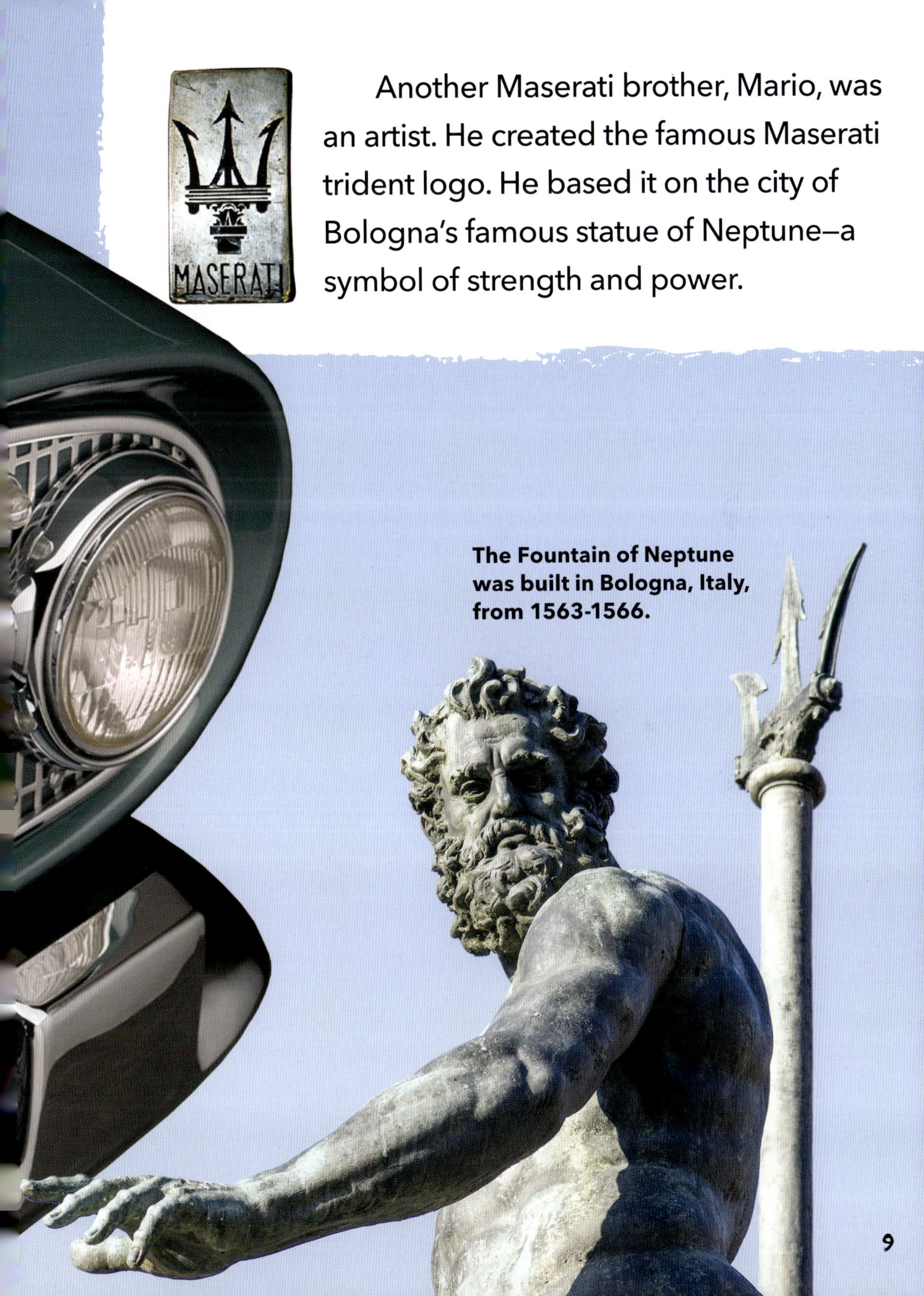

Another Maserati brother, Mario, was an artist. He created the famous Maserati trident logo. He based it on the city of Bologna's famous statue of Neptune—a symbol of strength and power.

The Fountain of Neptune was built in Bologna, Italy, from 1563-1566.

In 1932, Alfieri died during surgery to repair racing-related injuries. Other Maserati brothers continued running the company until 1937. Businessman Adolfo Orsi bought Maserati and moved it to Modena, Italy. Over the years, Maserati had many different owners. Today, the Fiat Chrysler Automobiles group owns it. The factory remains in Modena.

XTREME FACT

In the 1970s, serious financial problems nearly caused Maserati to close forever. The Italian government stepped in to save the company and its many jobs until a new owner could be found.

MASERATI'S WINNING RACERS

Maserati celebrated many racing victories. In 1926, Baconi Borzacchini set a Class C car world land speed record of 152.9 mph (246.1 kph) in a Maserati Tipo 26. The record stood for nearly 10 years.

After a Maserati 8CTF won the 1939 Indy 500, a total of four racers competed driving Maserati 8CTFs the next year, but the Boyle Special was the 1940 winner.

In 1939 and 1940, American Wilbur Shaw won the **Indianapolis 500** driving a Maserati 8CTF known as the "Boyle Special." Ernesto Maserati designed the car for the Boyle Racing Team from Chicago, Illinois. No European car had won the Indy 500 since 1919. Maserati cars became known as winners.

The 1939 Boyle Special's average speed was 115 mph (185 kph).

In the 1950s, Maserati developed the 250F. Famous drivers Stirling Moss of Great Britain and Argentina's Juan Manuel Fangio chose it as their **Formula One** racer.

Moss drove the Maserati 250F to win the 1956 Italian Grand Prix. In 1957, Fangio raced the 250F to win the German Grand Prix at **Nürburgring**.

Stirling Moss and the 250F averaged 130 mph (209 kph) over 50 laps of the 1956 Italian Grand Prix.

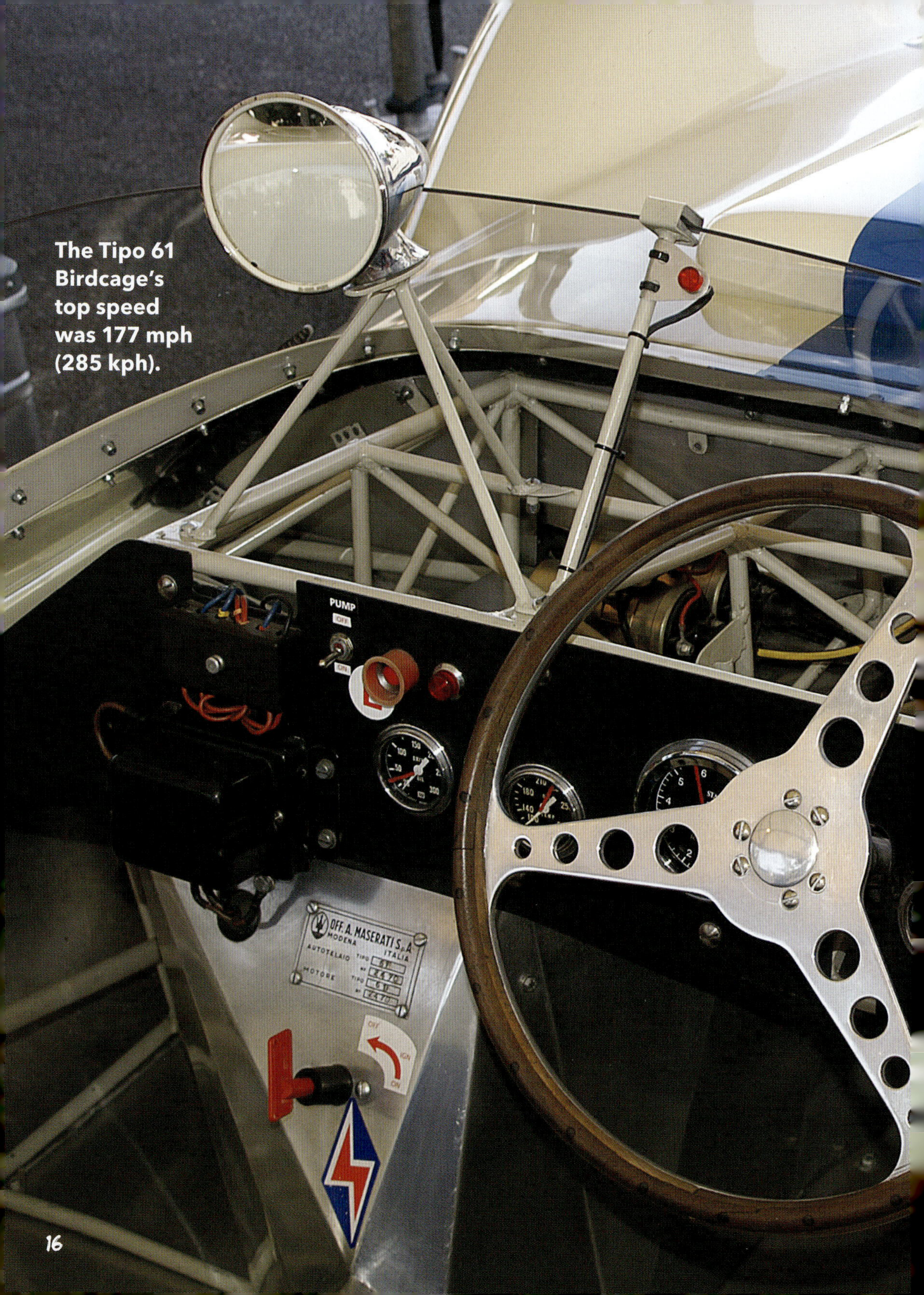

The Tipo 61
Birdcage's
top speed
was 177 mph
(285 kph).

Engineer Giulio Alfieri wanted something new for Maserati. He welded together 200 small-section tubes to create the Tipo 60 and 61 models. The style became known as the "Birdcage." America's Camoradi racing team took their Birdcage to wins at the 1960 and 1961 **Nürburgring** 1000 km.

CHAPTER 4

GRAN TURISMO TOURING CAR

Maserati's first **production car** was the 1500 GranTurismo. The 1947 grand touring car featured a race car engine in a **luxury** coupe.

1500 GranTurismo

More than 70 years after Maserati's first model, today's GranTurismo continues to mix cool style with surging power. Its impressive V8 engine has a legendary sound. Its top speed is 186 mph (300 kph).

The GranTurismo combines modern technology with a classic leather interior. A 8.4-inch (21-cm) touchscreen display puts controls at the driver's fingertips. Hand-stitched details and the trident **logo** show the **luxury** of a Maserati.

GranTurismo Sport

CHAPTER 5

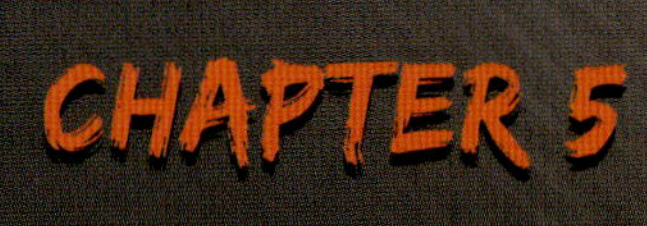

QUATTROPORTE SPORTS SEDAN

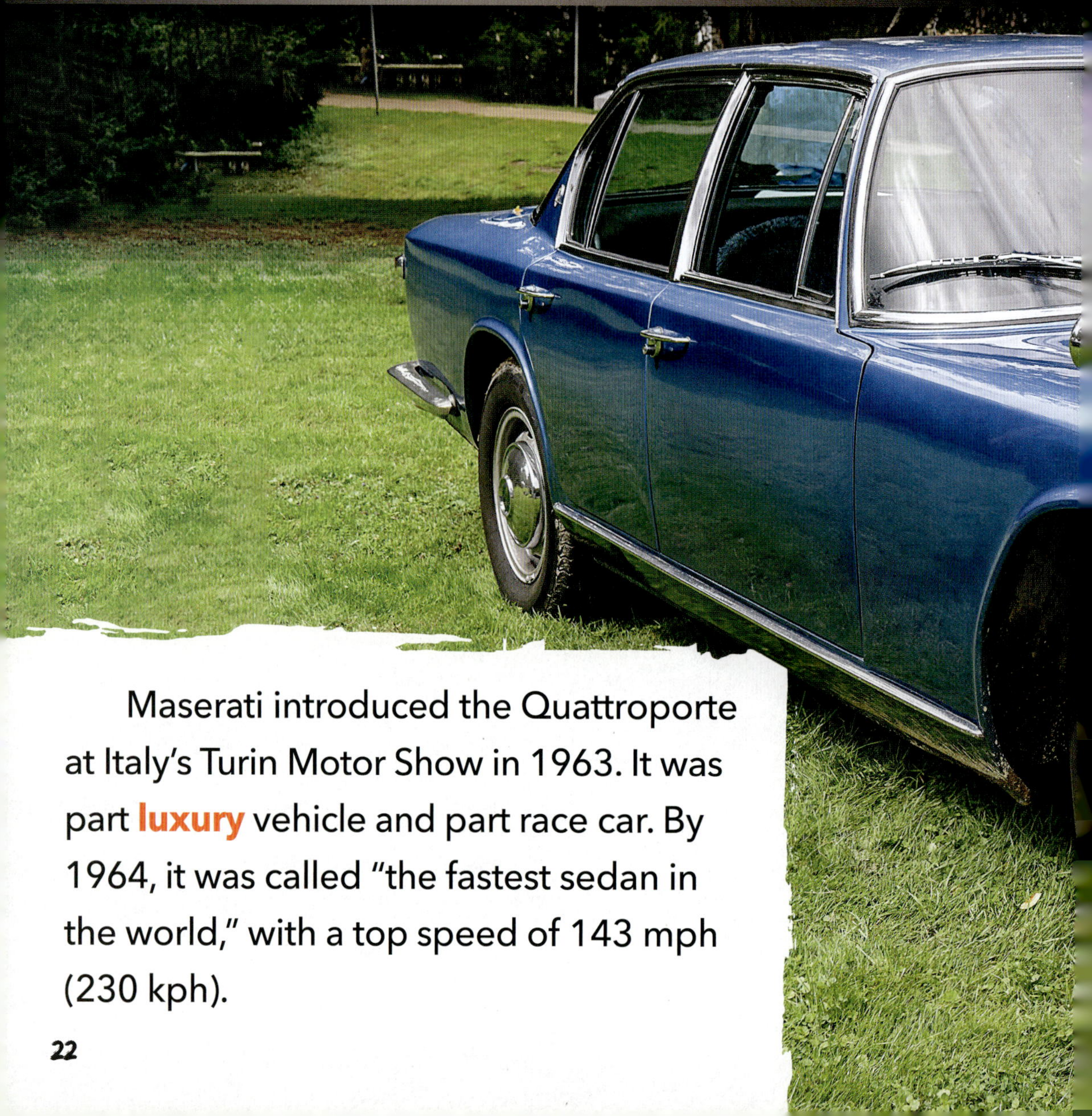

Maserati introduced the Quattroporte at Italy's Turin Motor Show in 1963. It was part **luxury** vehicle and part race car. By 1964, it was called "the fastest sedan in the world," with a top speed of 143 mph (230 kph).

Quattroporte is the Italian word for "four doors." This is a regular feature on sedans.

QUATTROPORTE SPECIFICATIONS

YEARS PRODUCED
1963-Present

MAXIMUM HORSEPOWER
580 (2021 Trofeo model)

ZERO TO 60 MPH (97 KPH)
4.2 seconds (Trofeo model)

There have been six generations of Quattroporte. The **luxury** sedan usually came with a powerful V8 engine, but beginning in 2013, a **Ferrari** twin-turbo V6 became standard. The 2021 Quattroporte Trofeo ("trophy") brought back the V8 option, creating a blinding top speed of 203 mph (326 kph).

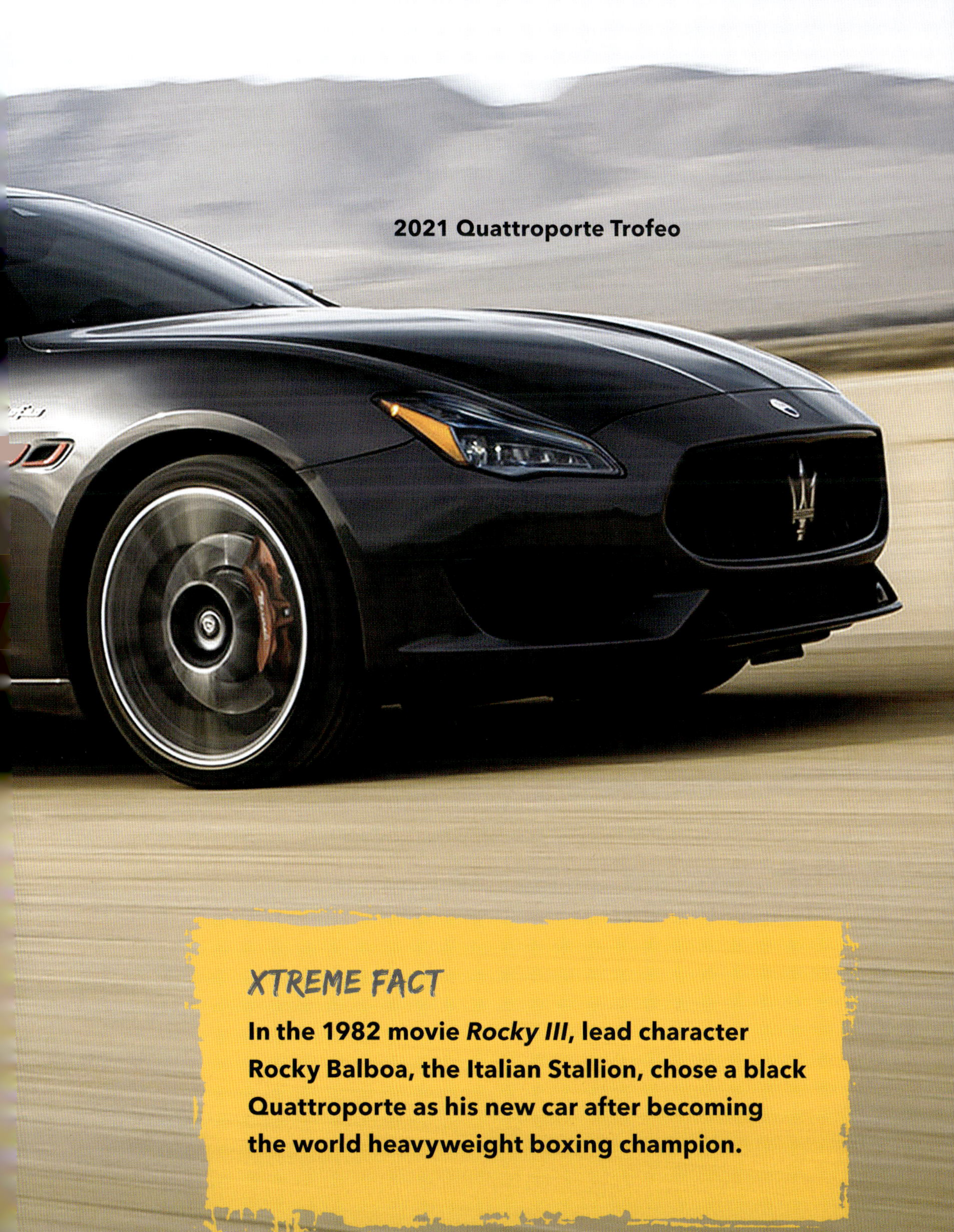

2021 Quattroporte Trofeo

XTREME FACT

In the 1982 movie *Rocky III*, lead character Rocky Balboa, the Italian Stallion, chose a black Quattroporte as his new car after becoming the world heavyweight boxing champion.

CHAPTER 6

GHIBLI GT SPORTS CAR

The Ghibli (gib-blee) was introduced in 1966. Auto designer Giorgetto Giugiaro created this GT (grand tourer) sports car with a steel body, long nose, and V8 engine. It went 0-60 mph (97 kph) in 6.8 seconds, competing with rivals **Ferrari** and Lamborghini.

Ghibli's design was part of the Wedge Era. Designer Giugiaro created these sharp-lined, wedge-shaped vehicles for Maserati, Lotus, DeLorean, and others.

A V8 engine gives the Ghibli Trofeo race-inspired power.

Today's Ghibli features a clean, **aerodynamic** shape. With a standard V6 engine, it reaches a top speed of 178 mph (286 kph). The Trofeo V8 model speeds up to 203 mph (326 kph). The Ghibli GT hybrid is Maserati's first all-electric vehicle. It reaches 158 mph (255 kph).

XTREME FACT

Maserati named many of its vehicles after various words for wind. Ghibli is a "hot, dust-carrying desert wind" in North Africa.

BORA ROAD CAR

Bora was Maserati's first mid-mounted, rear-engine road car, introduced in 1971. Also designed by Giorgetto Giugiaro, the wedge-shaped supercar had all-steel side panels and a stainless steel roof. Bora provided drivers with performance, safety, and comfort. Its top speed was 177 mph (285 kph).

BORA SPECIFICATIONS
YEARS PRODUCED
1971-1980
MAXIMUM HORSEPOWER
330 (Bora 4.9)
ZERO TO 60 MPH (97 KPH)
6.2 seconds (Bora 4.9)
Bora is named after a wind that blows from the Adriatic Sea and is felt in Trieste, Italy.

Bora's steering wheel tilted
up and down and telescoped
in and out.

The two-person Bora had leather bucket seats. The driver adjusted the driving position by moving the steering wheel and pedal box (clutch, brake, and accelerator pedals), instead of the seat. Pressing a button moved the pedal box forward or backward a maximum of 3 inches (8 cm).

CHAPTER 8

SPYDER OPEN TOP CAR

Maserati's 1984 Spyder offered drivers an open top for the first time since the early 1970s. Early models of the **luxury** two-seater had a V6, twin-turbo engine. When **fuel injection** was introduced, the Spyder i models reached a top speed of 143 mph (230 kph).

SPYDER SPECIFICATIONS

YEARS PRODUCED
1984-2007

MAXIMUM HORSEPOWER
390 (2006 Spyder)

ZERO TO 60 MPH (97 KPH)
4.6 seconds (2006 Spyder)

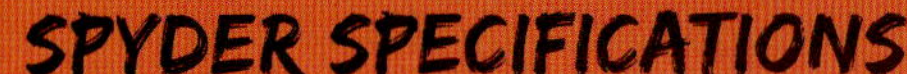

A Spyder's beautiful leather interior featured a gold watch on the dashboard.

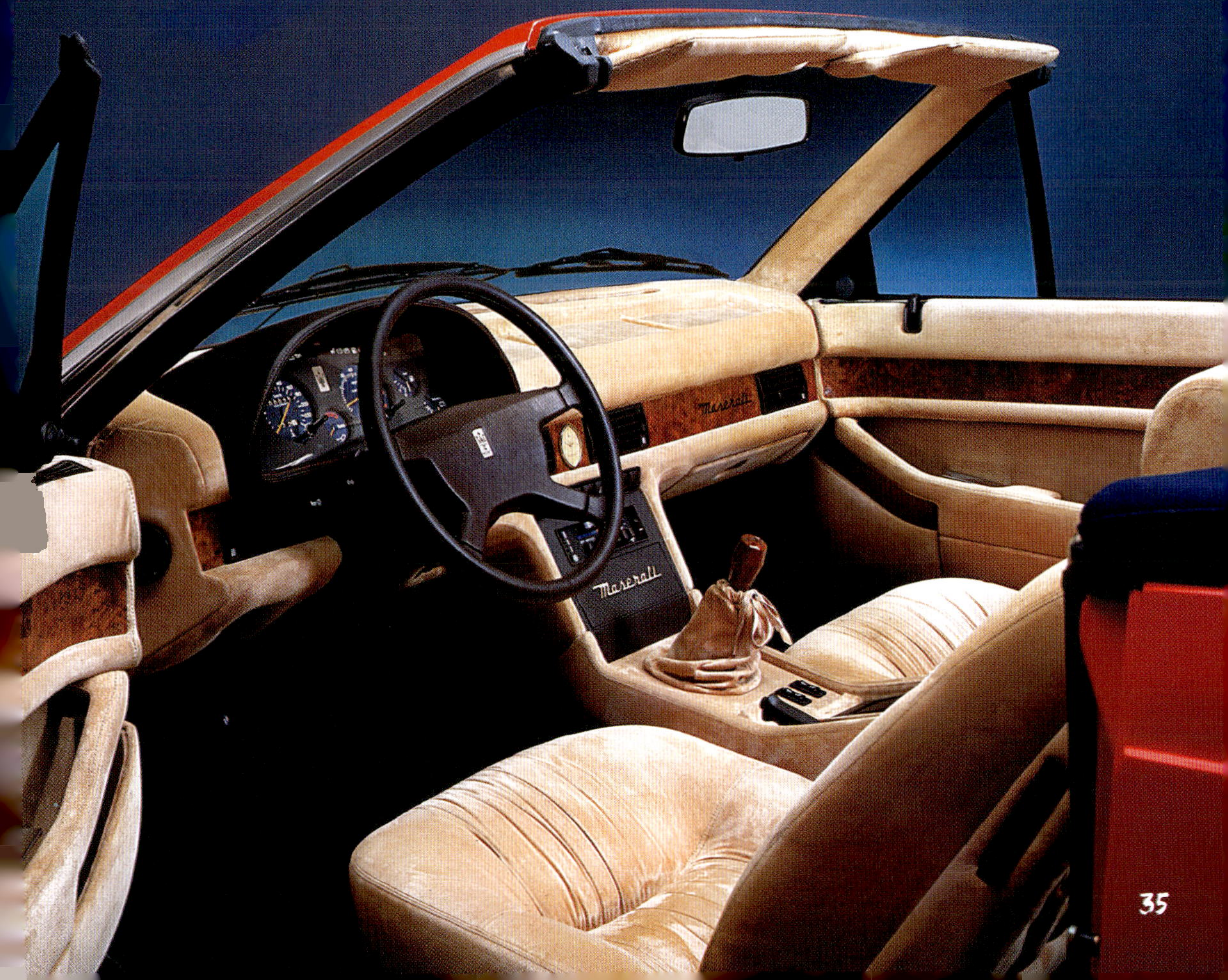

The Maserati Spyder underwent a major redesign in the early 2000s. The sleek, beautiful convertible featured a powerful V8 **Ferrari** engine that brought the Spyder's top speed to 176 mph (283 kph).

The redesigned Maserati Spyder had several safety features including front and side air bags and roll bars behind each seat.

XTREME FACT

Long-time rival car companies Maserati and
Ferrari were joined in partnership in 1993.
Both became divisions of Fiat. Afterwards,
Maserati cars were made with Ferrari engines.

CHAPTER 9

MASERATI MC CARS

MC (Maserati Corse) vehicles are sports cars built for racing. The MC12 supercar was first built in 2004-2005. It was designed to compete in the FIA GT Championship, bringing Maserati back to racing after 37 years.

The MC12 came in three colors: white with blue detailing, carbon blue, and a single car that was made in black.

The MC12 is the fastest Maserati road car ever built with a top speed of 205 mph (330 kph).

Maserati's MC20 features a new high-tech, ultra-light carbon fiber body. Combined with a high-performance V6 Nettuno engine, the Italian design is stronger, faster, and safer.

The MC20 has a mid-engine design. It is placed behind the sports car's two seats.

The MC20 is the first Maserati with butterfly wing doors. They are designed to make it easier to get in and out of the car.

The MC20 has a carbon fiber steering wheel.

The MC20 is racetrack ready. It is also designed with the comfort a driver needs for long-distance travel.

CHAPTER 10

THE FUTURE

Future Maseratis will merge electric power with Italian beauty and speed. Hybrid technology is being developed with a new electric Folgore (Italian for "lightning") **drivetrain**. Maserati will bring modern and streetwear design to its famous automobiles.

Maserati and Fragment Design creator Hiroshi Fujiwara of Japan have developed a special edition Ghibli.

**TAKE THE QUIZ BELOW AND
PUT WHAT YOU'VE LEARNED TO THE TEST!**

1) Who started the Maserati company? In what year?

2) The Maserati trident logo is very famous. Who developed it and where did the idea come from?

3) What model of Maserati set a Class C world land speed record? Who was the driver? How long did the record stand?

4) Engineer Giulio Alfieri welded together 200 small-section tubes creating the unique Tipo 60 and 61 race cars. What were these cars nicknamed?

5) What was Maserati's first production car?

6) What model of Maserati was called "the fastest sedan in the world?"

7) What does MC stand for? What are these supercars designed to do?

GLOSSARY

aerodynamic – Something that has a shape that reduces the drag, or resistance, of air moving across its surface. Sports cars with aerodynamic shapes can go faster because they don't have to push as hard to get through the air.

drivetrain – The parts of a motor vehicle connected to the engine that deliver power to the wheels to make the vehicle move.

Ferrari – An Italian automobile manufacturer, originally begun by Enzo Ferrari in 1939. Ferraris are expensive luxury sports and racing cars.

Formula One (F1) – A single-seat, super-fast racing vehicle. F1 cars are typically raced on racetracks or road courses.

fuel injection – A system that mixes air and a fine spray of gasoline into an engine cylinder. Instead of using suction to draw in the gasoline, like a carburetor, fuel injection uses a small nozzle to spray gas under pressure directly into the cylinder.

Grand Prix – A single-seat racing car with uncovered wheels.

Indianapolis 500 – A popular automobile race that takes place every May in Speedway, Indiana. The race lasts 200 laps. It is called the "500" because 200 times around the track equals 500 miles (805 km).

logo – A graphic symbol that identifies a company.

luxury – Something that adds pleasure or comfort, and is often expensive.

Nürburgring – A famous racetrack in Nürburg, Germany, that opened in 1927. Also called "The Ring," it is considered one of the most challenging racetracks in the world.

production car – A model of car that is produced by a company that all look the same and are sold to the public.

spark plug – A device used to produce a spark that ignites a fuel mixture, usually gasoline, in an engine.

ONLINE RESOURCES

To learn more about Maserati, please visit **abdobooklinks.com** or scan this QR code. These links are routinely monitored and updated to provide the most current information available.